HAND GAMES

Mario Mariotti

Made possible

by a donation

from the

Thomas M. Kirbo & Irene B. Kirbo
Charitable Trust

1995
1995

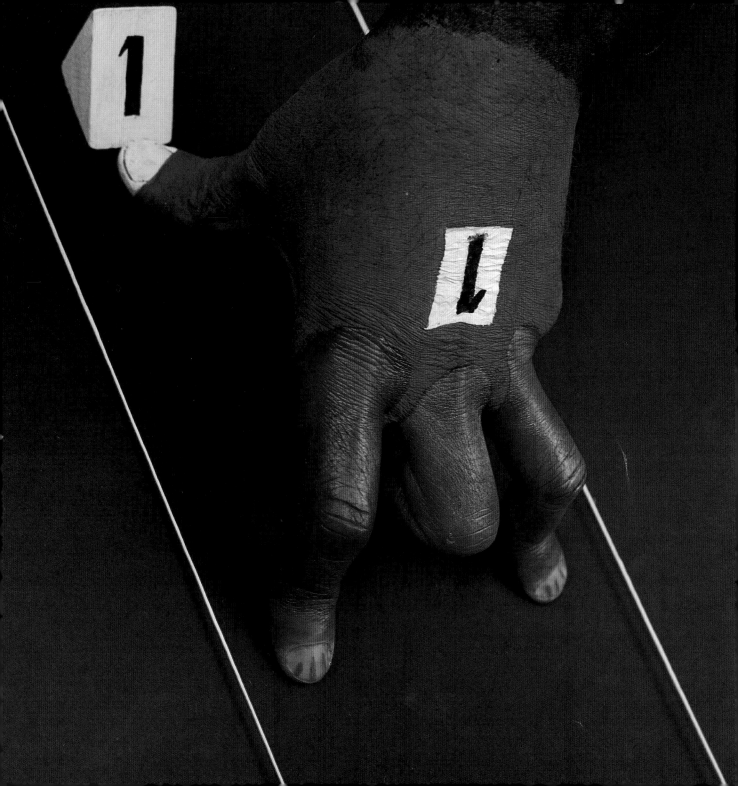

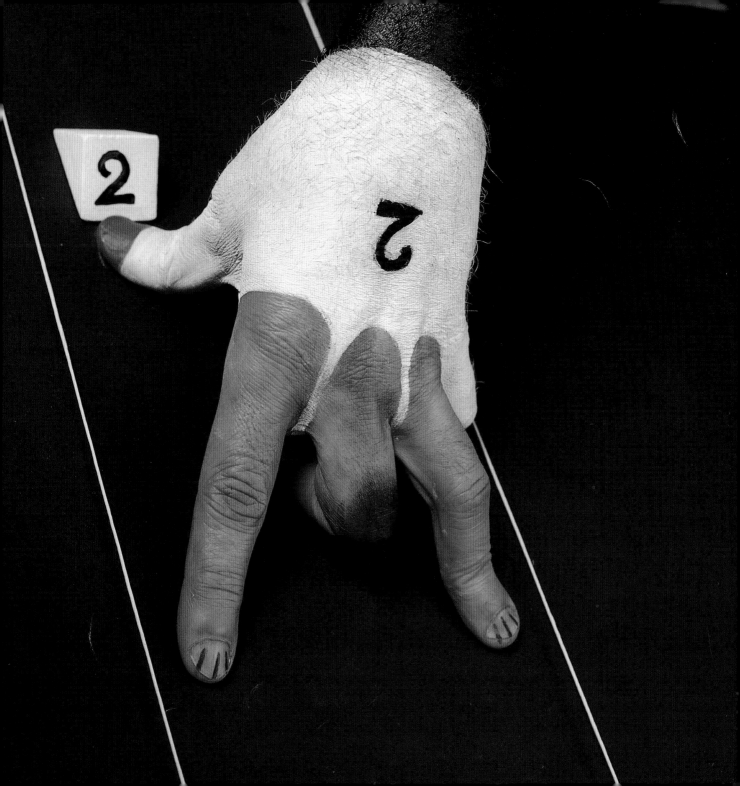

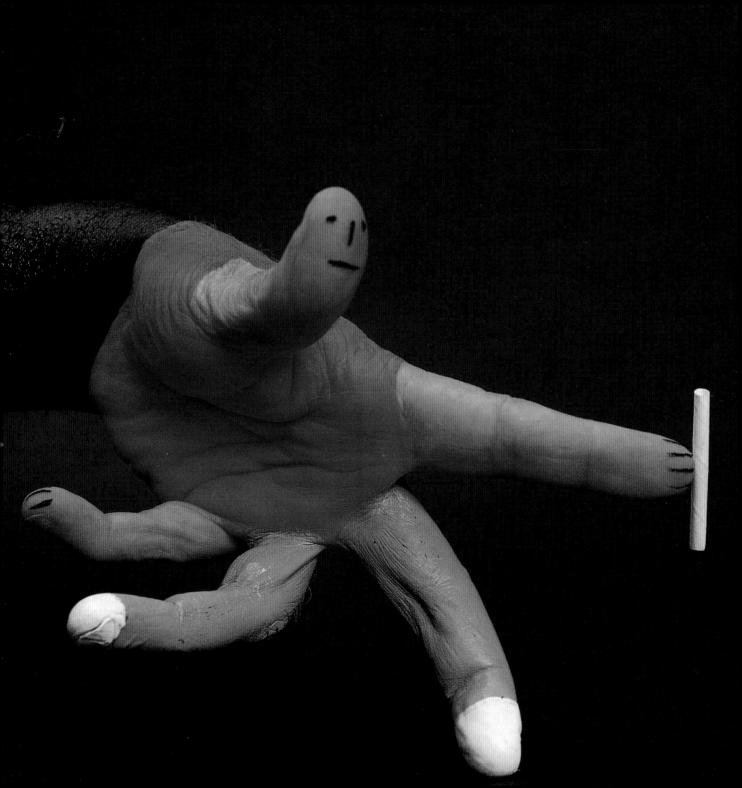

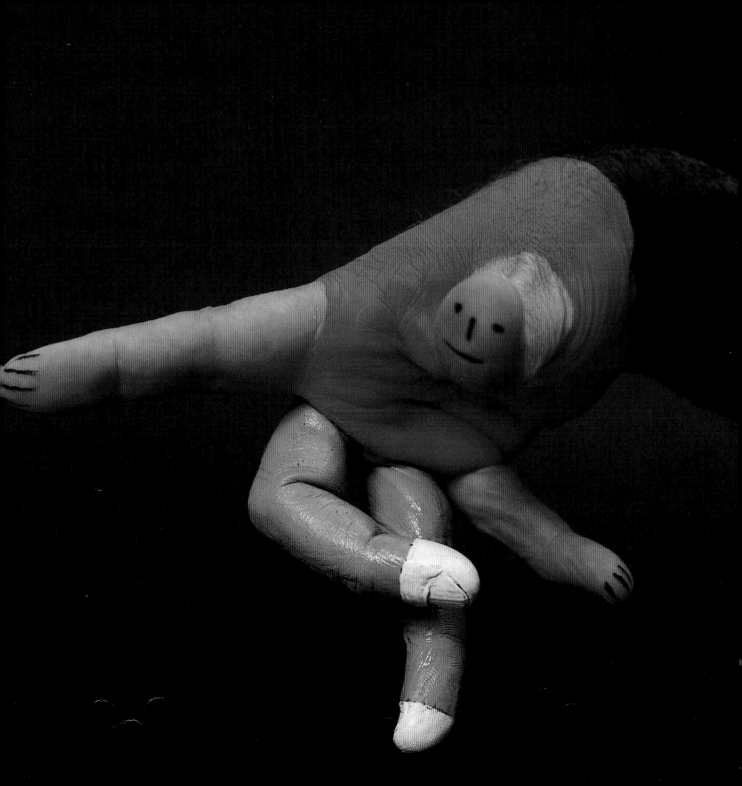

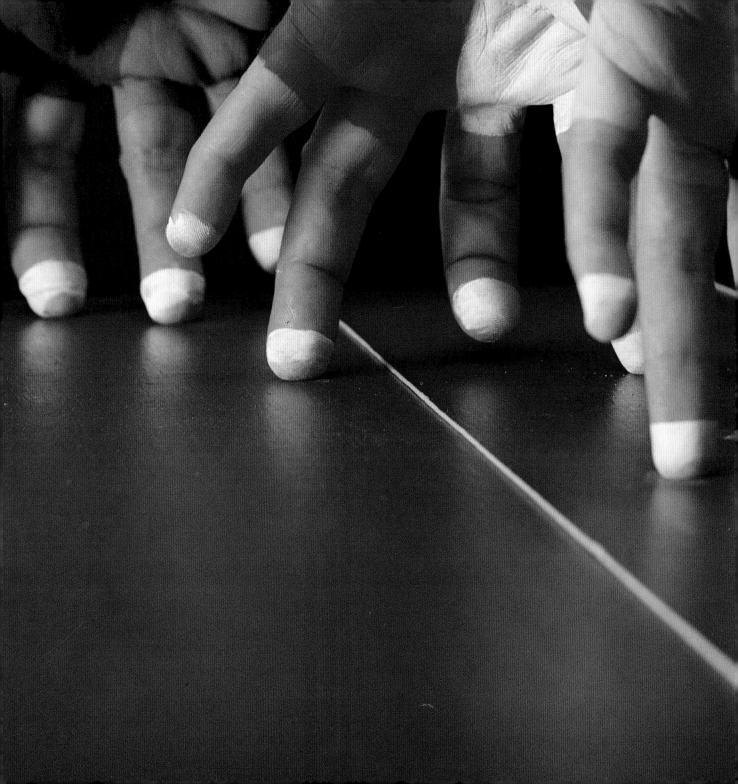

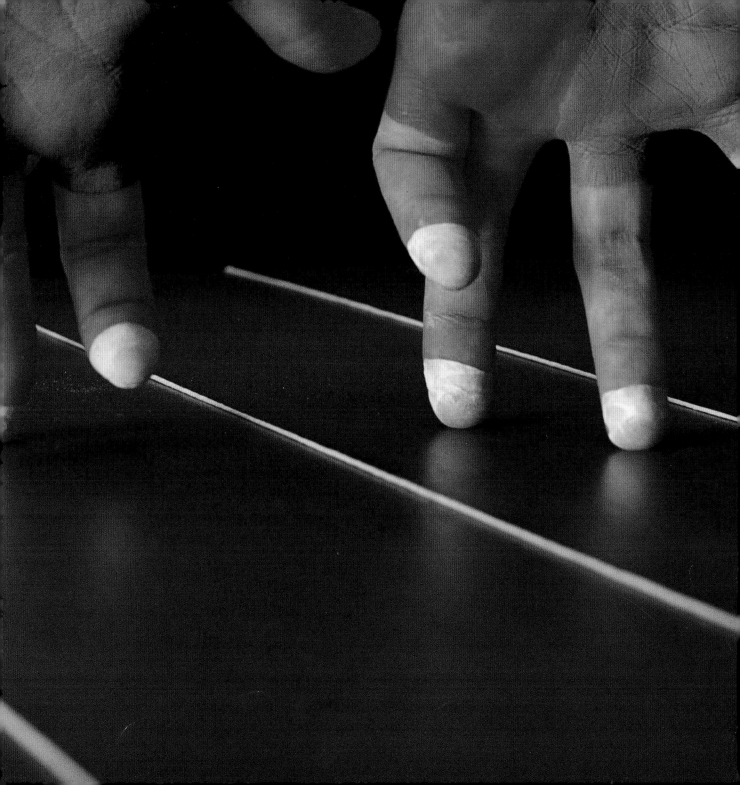

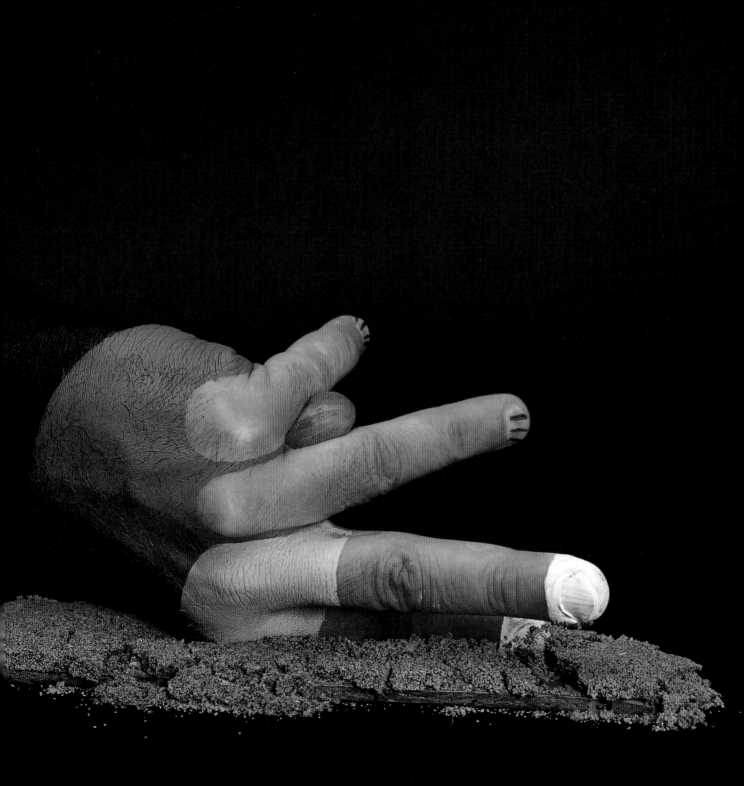

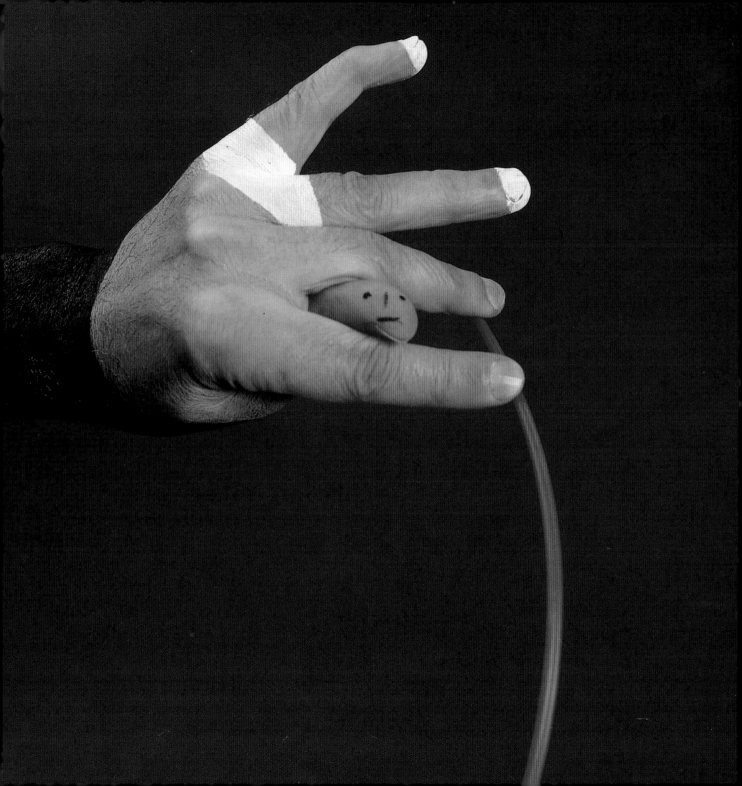

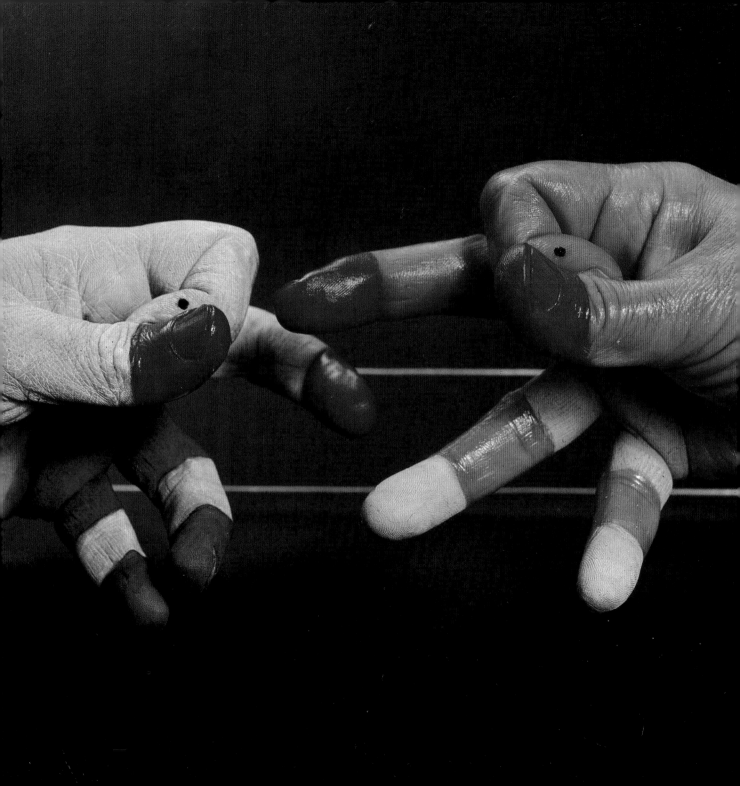

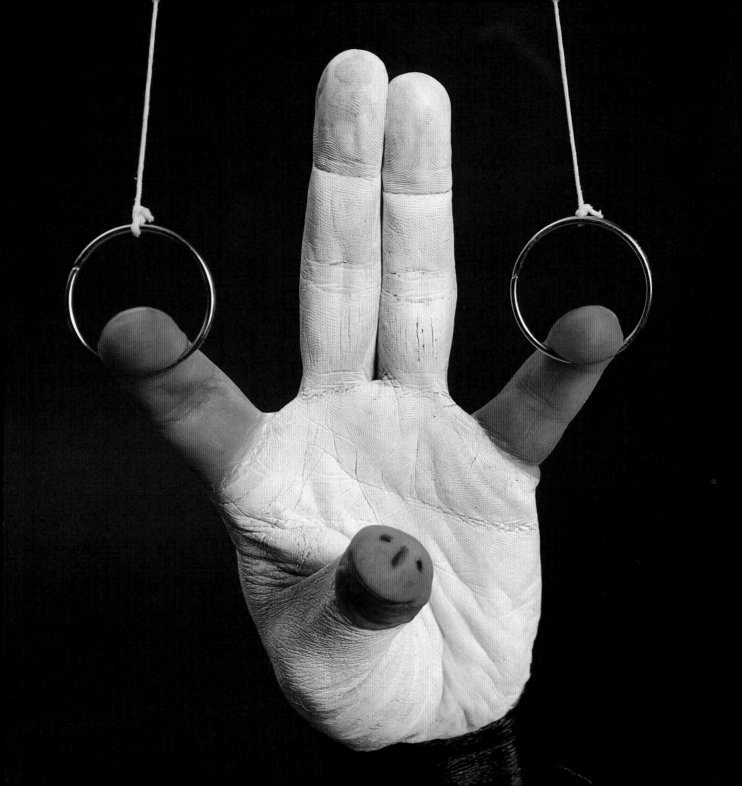

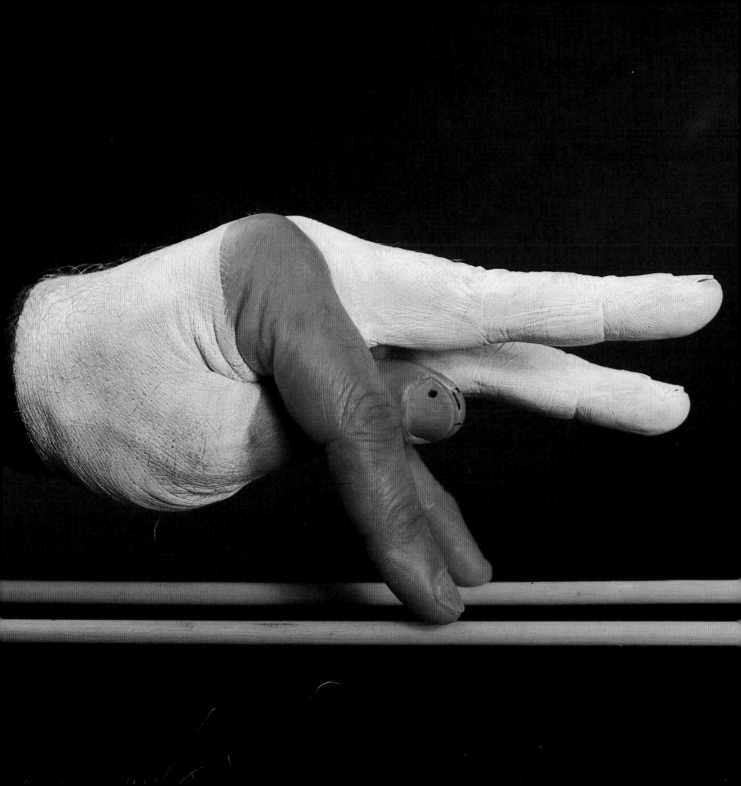

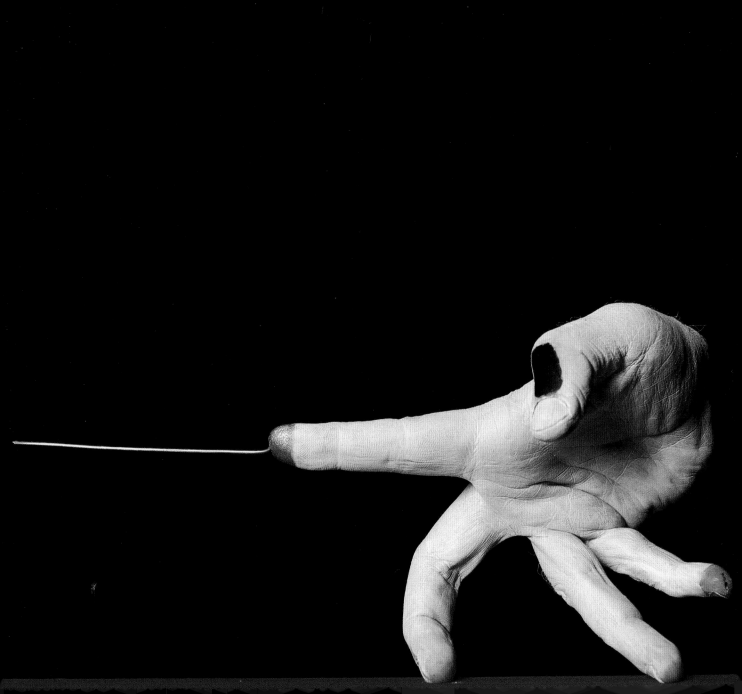

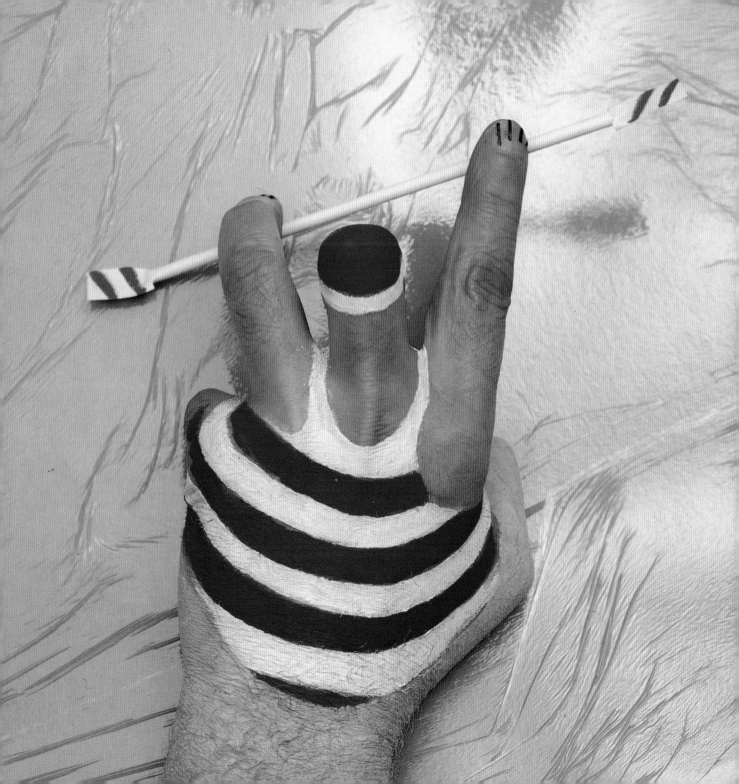

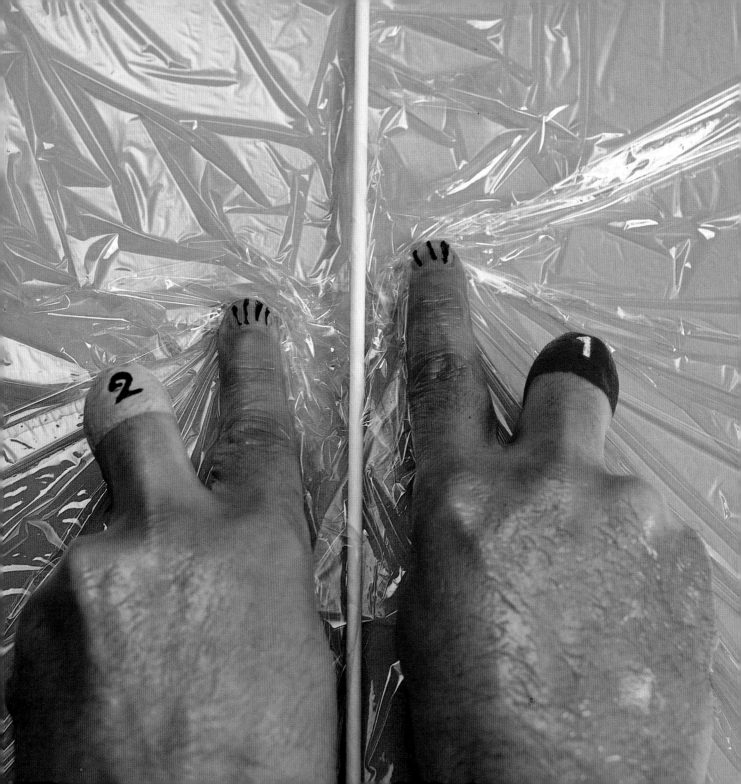

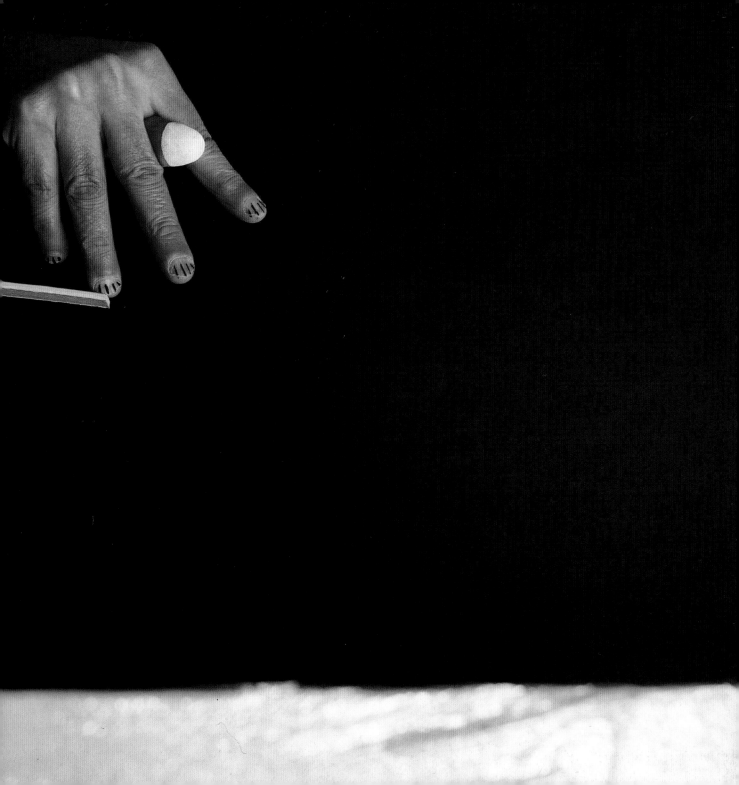

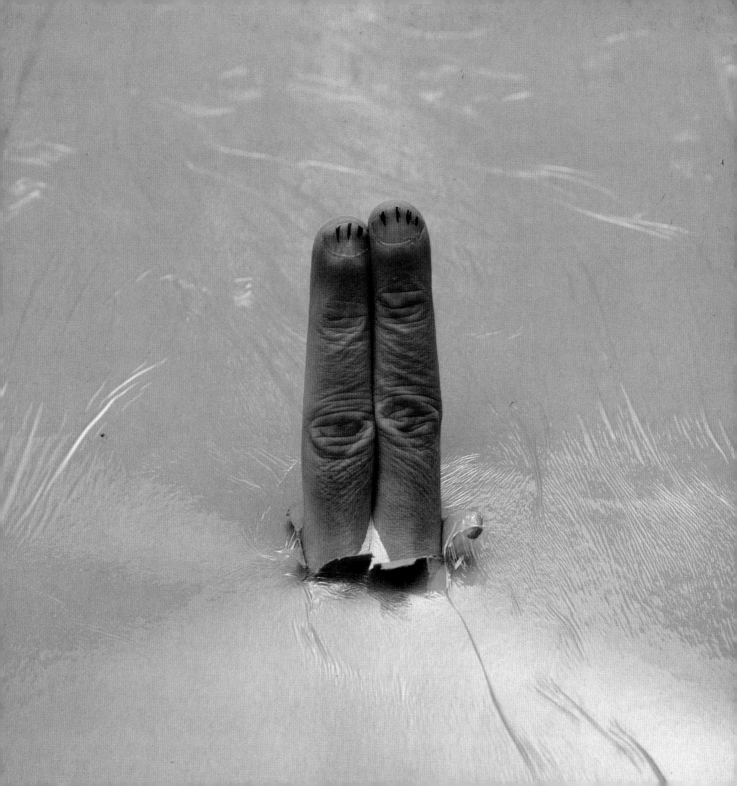

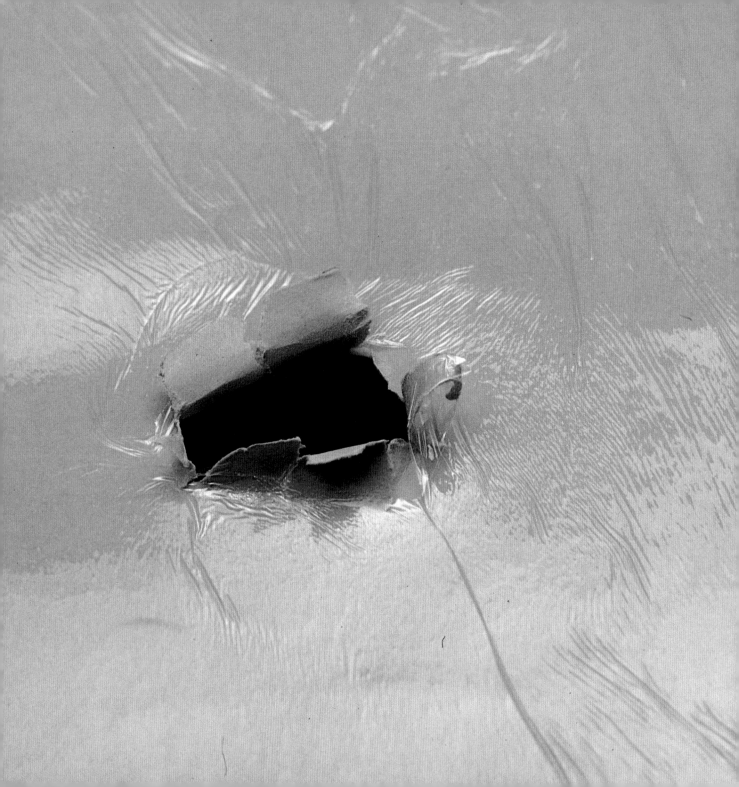

Hands, by their very nature, are not always such good sports. They won't always play the game, or rather, they will but only in their own way.

The feet, of course, know all about this, for in most sports competitions, they wind up doing most of the work, while the hands get most of the glory. Even in victory, although the feet get to climb the winner's stand, it is merely to enable the hands to raise themselves to the sky in celebration.

More down to earth, the humble feet hurt from exertion and swell and swelter inside hot athletic shoes where they must gasp for breath. Meanwhile, the joyful hands, out in the fresh air, gather in all the accolades—shaking hands still warm from applause, signing autographs and gathering in bouquets, trophies, medals, citations and whatever else comes their way.

And that's what these HAND GAMES are like. "Give us a sturdy pedestal and a good photographer, and we'll be there with a ready pose." So say the vainglorious hands!

MARIO MARIOTTI